# DR. K.
## PROFESSIONAL TH

created by **Jonathan Katz** and **Tom Snyder**

written by **Bill Braudis**
illustrated by **Dick Truxaw**

MW01077726

# Hey, I've Got My Own Problems

POCKET BOOKS

New York   London   Toronto   Sydney   Tokyo   Singapore

An *Original* Publication of POCKET BOOKS

POCKET BOOKS, a division of Simon & Schuster Inc.
1230 Avenue of the Americas, New York, NY 10020

Copyright © 1997 by Comedy Central. All rights reserved.

The Dr. Katz comic strip is distributed by the *Los Angeles Times* Syndicate.

ISBN: 0-671-00758-0

First Pocket Books trade paperback printing October 1997

10 9 8 7 6 5 4 3 2

Pocket and colophon are registered trademarks of Simon & Schuster Inc.

Printed in the U.S.A.

*To Loren Bouchard*

For orders other than by individual consumers, Pocket Books grants a discount on the purchase of 10 or more copies of single titles for special markets or premium use. For further details, please write to the Vice-President of Special Markets, Pocket Books, 1633 Broadway, New York, NY 10019-6785 8th Floor.

For information on how individual consumers can place orders, please write to Mail Order Department, Simon & Schuster Inc., 200 Old Tappan Road, Old Tappan, NJ 07675.

# Acknowledgments

Introduction written by Jonathan Wilson
Cover Design by Comedy Central

Special thanks at Comedy Central to: Jason Huffman, Larry Lieberman, Frank Quinn, Vinnie Sainato

Special thanks at The Los Angeles Times Syndicate to: Steve Christensen, Cathy Irvine, Jesse Levine, Jim Lomenzo

Special thanks at The Retro Ranch to: Melissa Bardin, Annette LeBlanc Cate, Niki Hebert

Special thanks at Pocket Books to: Lynda Castillo, Joann Foster, Max Greenhut, Donna O'Neill, Donna Ruvituso, Liate Stehlik, Dave Stern, Kara Welsh

VISIT WITH DR. KATZ ON THE COMEDY CENTRAL WEBSITE:
www.comedycentral.com

# Introduction

Dr. Katz, America's most popular therapist, has made the transition—or as he might call it, transference—from animated television to comic-strip form. The trauma doesn't seem to have affected his trademark low-key, deadpan analyses or the wonderfully comic and neurotic manias, phobias, fixations, fetishes and crazes of his patients. Here, in Bill Braudis's words and Dick Truxaw's illustrations, Laura, the doctor's hot-looking receptionist (voiced on TV by actress Laura Silverman), is as caustic as ever, and Ben (actor H. Jon Benjamin), his twenty-four-year-old son, an aspiring underachiever, is as frustrating, frustrated, hypochondriacal, lovable and big-luggable as when he first appeared on TV unemployed and apparently unemployable.

*Dr. Katz Professional Therapist,* is, of course, the brainchild of comedian, actor, writer Jonathan Katz and his partner, Tom Snyder, the creator of the program's hallmark animated vibrations known as Squigglevision. It began as a five-minute tape called "The Biography of Mr. Katz," which, after Comedy Central had enthusiastically stepped in, quickly developed into the half-hour *Dr. Katz,* and the rest is animated television history. The TV show has now been running on Comedy Central with huge success through four seasons. Dr. Katz has won an Emmy and two Cable Ace awards, and, as far as his reputation is concerned, it seems as if half the arts and entertainment world want to be his patient.

Winona Ryder, or her animated image, has spilled her guts, and so has Pulitzer-winning playwright David Mamet; Gary Shandling wants Dr. Katz to help him deal with his attraction to older women, while Lisa Kudrow needs some assertiveness training to help her cope with an obnoxious colleague. The list goes on: Rita Rudner, Janeane Garofalo, Steven Wright, Joan Rivers, Sandra Bernhard, Ray Romano, and Rodney Dangerfield. They all need straightening out. But why do they choose to lie on Dr. Katz's comfy couch? After all, big cities are full of therapists ready to relieve you of a hundred and fifty bucks minimum for a fifty-minute session.

The answer seems to lie in the deep admiration his patients have for Dr. Katz's empathetic character ("I think that you really have tapped into something special," says Sandra Bernhard. "You're not detached, you're not caught up in the whole stardom of being a therapist.") and their equally profound misconception of his method. While his patients think Dr. Katz is taking notes, he is, in fact, frequently doodling. While they believe he is concentrating on their problems, he is usually worrying about his own, or associating to memories of his own childhood.

In fact, the characters who receive most of his serious attention are not his famous and needy patients, but rather Ben, Laura and the doctor's friends at the local bar where he unwinds. Nursing his imported beer at Jacky's 33 Bar, Katz can relax after a long day's grueling work listening to Dom Irrera fantasize about how he and the doctor might ride each other "like two Vikings—but not in a gay way," or Joy Behar decrying his physical appearance, particularly the length of his nose hairs, then adding as a culminating insult at the end of her session, "I find you repulsive." In the company of Julie (voiced by actress, Julianne Shapiro), the tolerant, reasonable, supportive bartender at Jacky's 33, and his good buddy Stanley (voiced by actor Will Lebow), who is corny beyond belief, full of peculiar and invented knowledge, but nevertheless well-meaning, Katz finds better listeners than he ever does on his daily slate of narcissistic patients—or "customers" as Ben likes to call them.

I asked Jonathan Katz, the real Jonathan Katz, who, as he himself has pointed out, resembles his psychiatrist creation in many ways—except that Dr. Katz is more animated—if he had modeled Dr. Katz on shrinks he had encountered in his life, and if so, what his own experience of therapy had been like? Here are his responses: "I imitated the style of one particular shrink I've known—no names—but after meeting other shrinks, it seems like they all have the same emotional range, which is. . .none. I mean how many ways can you say *mmmhmmm*? As for my own first encounter in therapy, well, I will always make a joke in order to make myself comfortable in any new situation. So when I met this guy for the first time I opened with what I consider to be my best joke. I said, 'I had dinner with my father last night and I made a classic Freudian slip. I meant to say "Can you pass me the salt please" but it came out "You ****, you ruined my childhood." And the shrink said, 'Would you like me to laugh at that?' And I said, 'Not if you can help it.' Which is how I feel about comedy in general. Anyway after a couple of sessions I tried to get some sense of how long he thought I would need to see him and he said, 'Jonathan, you have so many levels of pain and shame that it's very hard to predict something like this.' And I said, 'Jeez, can you be a little more upbeat about it?' I've seen other shrinks who have not been that supportive. I saw a guy recently and every week he opened up with 'Now what's the matter?' And anytime I talked about my childhood he said, 'Please let's not open that can of worms.'"

Despite his creator's difficulties with shrinks, Dr. Katz has become a popular figure in the therapeutic community, so much so that Jonathan Katz (unanimated) was recently invited to address the American Psychological Association during their annual convention in Toronto. Therapists love Dr. Katz because he gets to say the things they're not allowed to say, and because viewers get to see him at home interacting with his own family, and behaving in understandably human ways. He is the shrink as vulnerable human being, rather than the analytical, withdrawn, impersonal, Viennese-accented doctor so familiar to us from the world of cartoons. In fact, a great deal of Dr. Katz's appeal has to do with the way in which he takes on and surmounts the problems of single-parenting an eternally adolescent twenty-four-year-old son. The relationship between Dr. Katz and Ben is at the heart of both the show and the strip. Ben is a lovely, endearing lazybones, a kind of millennial, American, Generation Xer incapable of action despite his best intentions, and preferring to spend most of his time horizontal on a decidedly non-analytic couch. When Ben does rouse himself it is generally in pursuit of the unattainable Laura. Thankfully, Laura's indifference to his advances and her ruthless rejection of them appear to have no effect whatsoever on Ben's good nature. Indeed, it is this part of Ben's being that always manages to soften the doctor's heart, even when he is being sorely tried by his son's indolence, or provoked by his outlandish business ventures. It is, after all, Ben who believes that a career as an "eyewitness" is feasible, and that, despite his major problems with arranging and keeping schedules, he is nevertheless well suited to life as a limo driver.

And what of Dr. Katz himself? What about his problems? He's divorced, lonely and phobic, and apparently finds it almost impossible to get a date. On the bright side, he's generally hopeful, upbeat and radiates a winning innocence in a crazy world. In times of personal trouble he can, of course, always take up his beloved guitar—and the doctor, as it turns out, sings rather sweetly. So here he is in his new comic-strip incarnation, framed but not confined, hilarious as usual, punchier than ever, in black and white on weekdays and color on Sundays, and with a whole new range of patients. Business is booming for Dr. Katz, and it is no longer only the famous and neurotic who have access to his couch. All manner of individuals, with a rainbow spectrum of personal problems, now run the gauntlet of Laura to seek the doctor's sympathetic ear. It's certainly worth it—although perhaps more for us than for them—and it's hard to say who's more disappointed, patients or fans, when Dr. Katz announces at the end of a session: "You know what the music means."

JONATHAN WILSON

HEY, KATZ. I GOT AN EXTRA TICKET TO THE HOCKEY GAME. YOU WANNA TO GO?

HOCKEY'S SUCH A VIOLENT SPORT.

HEY, I'M NOT ASKING YOU TO PLAY. I'M JUST ASKING IF YOU WANT TO SWEAR AT SOME PLAYERS.

IT DOESN'T INTEREST ME. SEE, I LIKE GOLF.

I DIDN'T KNOW YOU GOLFED?

YOU KIDDING? FOR ME, IT'S LIKE A RELIGION.

2-7

REALLY?

YEAH, I PLAY TWICE A YEAR.

BRAUDIS + TRUXAW

© 1997 Comedy Partners. Dist. Los Angeles Times Syndicate

YOU'RE PROBABLY WONDERING WHY I'M WEARING THIS DISGUISE, HUH?

NO.

IT'S MY FIRST TIME SEEING A THERAPIST AND I FEEL A LITTLE FUNNY ABOUT IT. I KNOW I SHOULDN'T. THERE'S NOTHING WRONG WITH IT.

BRAUDIS + TRUXAW

I MEAN, WHAT DO I CARE IF PEOPLE SEE ME COME IN HERE. YOU KNOW, I DON'T THINK I NEED TO WEAR A DISGUISE ANYMORE.

THERE, I FEEL MUCH BETTER.

2-8

© 1997 Comedy Partners. Dist. Los Angeles Times Syndicate

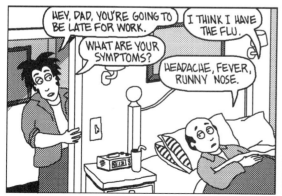

HI, LAURA, IT'S BEN. DON'T HANG UP. I'VE GOT SOME GOOD NEWS AND BAD NEWS.

THE BAD NEWS IS: MY DAD'S GOT THE FLU AND CAN'T WORK TODAY. WHAT? THAT'S GOOD NEWS? OH... I SEE.

2-12

WELL, IF THAT'S THE GOOD NEWS, THEN THE BAD NEWS IS: HE'S STILL GOING TO PAY YOU FOR THE DAY.

OH, RIGHT. GOOD NEWS, AGAIN. I SEE WHAT YOU'RE SAYING. SO IT WAS SORT OF A GOOD NEWS / GOOD NEWS... HELLO? HELLO?

© 1997 Comedy Partners. Dist Los Angeles Times Syndicate

BRAUDIS + TRUXAW

www.comedycentral.com

CAN I HELP YOU?

YES, I'D LIKE THE DOCTOR TO HAVE A LOOK AT MY CAT.

2-13

YOU HAVE THE WRONG PLACE, MA'AM. DR. KATZ IS A THERAPIST. FOR PEOPLE.

OH, I'M SORRY. I THOUGHT "DR. KATZ" WAS JUST A CLEVER LITTLE NAME FOR A VETERINARIAN.

© 1997 Comedy Partners. Dist Los Angeles Times Syndicate

OTHER PEOPLE HAVE SAID THAT TOO, BUT USUALLY AFTER THEIR FIRST SESSION.

BRAUDIS + TRUXAW

HEY, DAD, GOOD NEWS. I'M GOING TO INTERVIEW AT THE VIDEO STORE FOR THE ASSISTANT MANAGER'S POSITION.

WOW, THAT'S GREAT, BEN.

THANKS. I'M REALLY GOING TO PREPARE FOR IT. GET A NEW SUIT, A HAIRCUT, A PEDICURE...

2-21

AND WATCH EVERY VIDEO IN THE ENTIRE STORE. I'LL KNOW EVERYTHING THERE IS TO KNOW ABOUT MOVIES.

THAT'S VERY THOROUGH, BEN, BUT WHEN'S THE INTERVIEW?

WITH ALL THESE VIDEOS TO WATCH, I FIGURE SOMETIME IN MY LATE 50S.

BRAUDIS+TRUXAW

THAT'S WHY I GAVE UP MY DENTAL PRACTICE.

EVERYONE ALWAYS COMPLAINING ABOUT THE PAIN. I TOLD THEM WHAT MY DENTIST USED TO TELL ME... "SHUT UP."

AND DENTISTS HAVE A VERY HIGH SUICIDE RATE. WHO NEEDS IT? THAT'S ALL BEHIND ME NOW.

OKAY, RINSE.

2-22

BRAUDIS+TRUXAW

© 1997 Comedy Partners. Dist Los. Angeles Times Syndicate

HEY, DAD? WHAT'S THE NAME OF THE FLORIST WHO GIVES YOU 10 PERCENT OFF?

I DON'T HAVE A FLORIST WHO GIVES ME 10 PERCENT OFF.

YOU'RE THINKING OF PEPE'S GARAGE, THEY GIVE ME A BREAK ON TUNE-UPS.

OH, YEAH, I GET THEM CONFUSED. WELL, I NEED A FLORIST.

FOR WHAT?

OH, YOU KNOW, SPECIAL DAY COMING UP.

www.comcentral.com

BENNY, MY SON, YOU SOUND A LITTLE SMITTEN.

YEAH, I WOKE UP WITH IT. I THINK IT'S GOING AROUND.

© 1997 Comedy Partners. Dist. Los Angeles Times Syndicate

HAPPY VALENTINE'S DAY
to: laura
from: a secret admirer, Ben.

BEN, I REALLY DON'T WANT YOU BUYING ME FLOWERS.

WHAT? BUY? FLOWERS? ME?

IT SORT OF GIVES ME THE CREEPS.

REALLY? WELL, HOW DO YOU FEEL ABOUT TUNE-UPS?

2-9

BRAUDIS-TRUXAW

DR. KATZ, I'M VERY EXCITED. THIS IS MY FIFTH WEEK OF NOT SMOKING.

WELL THAT'S WONDERFUL. CONGRATULATIONS.

YEAH, NOT BAD CONSIDERING MY FOURTH WEEK OF NOT SMOKING WAS JUST TWO YEARS AGO.

WHENEVER WE GET INTO AN ARGUMENT, MY WIFE ALWAYS CALLS FOR A "TIMEOUT."

SHE'S LIKE A REFEREE.

THAT'S ACTUALLY AN EXCELLENT METHOD OF SUCCESSFULLY WORKING THROUGH A CONFLICT.

BUT IT'S NOT THE TIME-OUTS THAT BOTHER ME, DR. KATZ...

IT'S BLOWING THAT WHISTLE AND WEARING THAT STRIPED SHIRT THAT I FIND SO ANNOYING.

BRAUDIS + TRUXAW